tack **splash** *maneuver bo*
uirm escape learn obey i
ll gallivant sn *l d*
e wonder resp *ck*
uirm escape **look** *learn i*
mplore sniff decorate dev
uver bother pose guard t
e squirm escape learn **sh**
travel devour improvise i
vect attack maneuver loo
e implore bond share de
maneuver guard **bond** *s*

D0481438

wonder nestle respect a
k share collect decorate s
chew celebrate guard thr
ecorate bother conquer h
bond look share collect s
celebrate grin improvise
onder respect attack mar
sniff travel devour decor
ill gallivant share collec
bother conquer wonder re
squirm escape learn esca
ew wonder thrill galliva

photographs by sharon beals

what puppies do

CHRONICLE BOOKS

SAN FRANCISCO

for sweet Sal, who must have been a wonderful puppy

Printed in Hong Kong.

ISBN 0-8118-2074-2

Library of Congress Cataloging-in-Publication Data available.

Book and cover design: Alfredo Gregory
Composition: Gregory Design

Distributed in Canada by Raincoast Books, 8680 Cambie Street, Vancouver, BC V6P 6M9

10   9   8   7   6   5   4   3   2   1

Chronicle Books
85 Second Street
San Francisco, CA 94105

Web Site: www.chronbooks.com

very new dogs   *Puppies, puppies, puppies! After spending the last few months following their careening attention spans and wobbly wanderings, crawling on my stomach and almost being driven to use "auto-focus," my impressions of them wiggle all over my memory and are about as hard to corral as a litter of Labs. I get mental yips of joy when I think of their condensed milk breath and those little stubby noses that all pups start out with no matter how pointy the genes. My brain smiles at their zealous explorations of their new world, their ferocious attacks on mere leaves, and how, when their last calorie is spent, they collapse almost anywhere into a pile of loose limbs and bare bellies.* ▪ *But is all this enough to explain the thrall that I share with even the most cynical? (The congratulations to the new owner that are only a few emotional decibels down from those awarded a new baby?) At first, puppies' appeal would seem to be simply their high amusement factor, which does account for a lot. But if it were just their comic antics, would we put up with sleepless nights and lonely shoes and months of paper training? Even if I add to the sum of their charms the way they inspire our tenderness with their sweet vulnerability and their unhinged enthusiasm, expressed by total tongue licks and full body wiggles?* ▪ *To be sure, all of the above does help to mitigate some of the aforementioned trials of puppyness, but I would like to add my own two cents as an amateur animal observer. I think that puppies create such emotional commotion because we see in them qualities that will emerge after the brief frolic of puppyhood. Once in a while, when they stop chewing, yelping, and chasing, we get a glimpse into their little puppy souls. What we see shining through are the beginnings of loyalty, trust, and, as I said in my first book,* What Dogs Do, *some very important wisdom. Qualities that I think are the essence of dog; qualities that start young and endure long after training and age have matured the wiggles into dignified wags.*

nestle

conquer

wonder

respect

attack

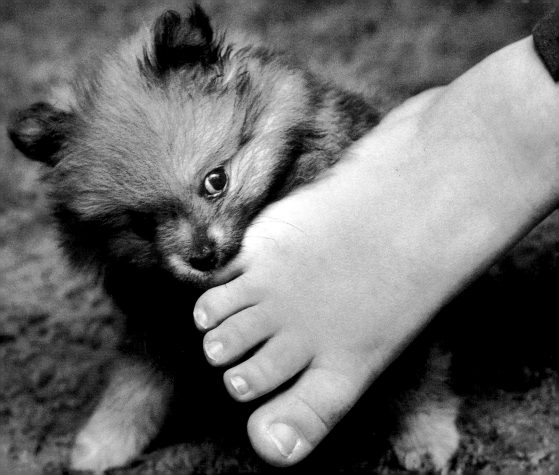

splash

maneuver

b o t h e r

pose

b   o   n   ∂

look

share

collect

decorate

squirm

e   s   c   a   p   e

learn

o   b   e   y

improvise

i m p l o r e

chew

celebrate

guard

grin

gallivant

travel

sniff

d e v o u r

h   o   p   e

wonder nestle respect a
share collect decorate s
ew celebrate guard th
orate bother conquer h
nd look share collect s
lebrate grin improvise
der respect attack ma
iff travel devour decor
gallivant share collec
ther conquer wonder r
uirm escape learn esc
wonder thrill galliva

my debts *to the people who have helped me along the way of making this small book are large and all too many to name. Here are just a few: my gratitude goes first to the keepers of all the many charming puppies that I photographed while working on this book. Your very generous time and help with the puppy wrangling was invaluable. I wish that the book could hold all of their antics. I owe Lynne at the Milo Foundation her own book, this time for letting me loose with her eager orphans. Thanks to Marty for darkroom salvation and to Sarah and Bernie for minding my critters during my many travels. My gratitude to Sandy at Serius Puppy Training and Gwen at Perfect Paws for letting me invade their classes. And to Sandy at Companion Dog Training for teaching me "basic dog." And finally, I must thank the rest of my friends who have fed me and editorialized during, and are still around after, this affair with a book.*

my debts *to the people who have helped me along the way of making this small book are large and all too many to name. Here are just a few: my gratitude goes first to the keepers of all the many charming puppies that I photographed while working on this book. Your very generous time and help with the puppy wrangling was invaluable. I wish that the book could hold all of their antics. I owe Lynne at the Milo Foundation her own book, this time for letting me loose with her eager orphans. Thanks to Marty for darkroom salvation and to Sarah and Bernie for minding my critters during my many travels. My gratitude to Sandy at Serius Puppy Training and Gwen at Perfect Paws for letting me invade their classes. And to Sandy at Companion Dog Training for teaching me "basic dog." And finally, I must thank the rest of my friends who have fed me and editorialized during, and are still around after, this affair with a book.*

tack **splash** maneuver bo
quirm escape learn obey in
ll gallivant sniff travel d
be wonder respect attack
quirm escape **look** learn in
mplore sniff decorate dev
uver bother pose guard t
e squirm escape learn **sh**
travel devour improvise i
pect attack maneuver loo
be implore bond share dec
maneuver guard **bond** s

wonder nestle respect a
k share collect decorate s
chew celebrate guard th
ecorate bother conquer h
bond look share collect s
celebrate grin improvise
onder respect attack mai
sniff travel devour decora
ill gallivant share collec
bother conquer wonder re
squirm escape learn esca
w wonder thrill galliva